THIS BOOK

BELONG TO:

 _____

_____

NOTES AND INTERESTING EVENTS:

_____
_____
_____
_____
_____
_____

BIRD PHOTO

BIRD SKETCH

DATE:

Day of the week: Time: Season:

AREA NAME:

Location: GPS COORDINATES:

HABITAT:	WEATHER CONDITIONS:

NAME OF BIRD:

Quantity Spotted: Time seen:

Location seen:	Sights, Activities Sounds When Seen:

Bird actions:

_____
_____
_____
_____
_____

BIRD DESCRIPTION:

species/ features/ markings

_____
_____
_____
_____
_____
_____
_____

NOTES AND INTERESTING EVENTS:

BIRD PHOTO

BIRD SKETCH

DATE:

Day of the week: Time: Season:

AREA NAME:

Location: GPS COORDINATES:

HABITAT:	WEATHER CONDITIONS:

NAME OF BIRD:

Quantity Spotted: Time seen:

Location seen:	Sights, Activities Sounds When Seen:

Bird actions:

_____

_____

_____

_____

_____

BIRD DESCRIPTION:
species/ features/ markings

_____

_____

_____

_____

_____

NOTES AND INTERESTING EVENTS:

BIRD PHOTO

BIRD SKETCH

DATE:

Day of the week: Time: Season:

AREA NAME:

Location: GPS COORDINATES:

HABITAT:	WEATHER CONDITIONS:

NAME OF BIRD:

Quantity Spotted: Time seen:

Location seen:	Sights, Activities Sounds When Seen:

Bird actions:

_____

_____

_____

_____

_____

BIRD DESCRIPTION:

species/ features/ markings

_____

_____

_____

_____

_____

_____

NOTES AND INTERESTING EVENTS:

BIRD PHOTO

BIRD SKETCH

DATE:

Day of the week: Time: Season:

AREA NAME:

Location: GPS COORDINATES:

HABITAT:	WEATHER CONDITIONS:

NAME OF BIRD:

Quantity Spotted: Time seen:

Location seen:	Sights, Activities Sounds When Seen:

Bird actions:

BIRD DESCRIPTION:

species/ features/ markings

NOTES AND INTERESTING EVENTS:

_____
_____
_____
_____
_____
_____

BIRD PHOTO

BIRD SKETCH

DATE:

Day of the week: Time: Season:

AREA NAME:

Location: GPS COORDINATES:

HABITAT:	WEATHER CONDITIONS:

NAME OF BIRD:

Quantity Spotted: Time seen:

Location seen:	Sights, Activities Sounds When Seen:

Bird actions:

_____

_____

_____

_____

_____

BIRD DESCRIPTION:

species/ features/ markings

_____

_____

_____

_____

_____

NOTES AND INTERESTING EVENTS:

BIRD PHOTO

BIRD SKETCH

DATE:

Day of the week: Time: Season:

AREA NAME:

Location: GPS COORDINATES:

HABITAT:	WEATHER CONDITIONS:

NAME OF BIRD:

Quantity Spotted: Time seen:

Location seen:	Sights, Activities Sounds When Seen:

Bird actions:

_____
_____
_____
_____
_____

BIRD DESCRIPTION:

species/ features/ markings

_____
_____
_____
_____
_____

_____
_____

NOTES AND INTERESTING EVENTS:

BIRD PHOTO

BIRD SKETCH

DATE:

Day of the week: Time: Season:

AREA NAME:

Location: GPS COORDINATES:

HABITAT:	WEATHER CONDITIONS:

<u>NAME OF BIRD</u>:

Quantity Spotted: Time seen:

Location seen:	Sights, Activities Sounds When Seen:

Bird actions:

BIRD DESCRIPTION:
species/ features/ markings

NOTES AND INTERESTING EVENTS:

BIRD PHOTO

BIRD SKETCH

DATE:

Day of the week: Time: Season:

AREA NAME:

Location: GPS COORDINATES:

HABITAT:	WEATHER CONDITIONS:

NAME OF BIRD:

Quantity Spotted: Time seen:

Location seen:	Sights, Activities Sounds When Seen:

Bird actions:

BIRD DESCRIPTION:

species/ features/ markings

NOTES AND INTERESTING EVENTS:

BIRD PHOTO

BIRD SKETCH

DATE:

Day of the week: Time: Season:

AREA NAME:

Location: GPS COORDINATES:

HABITAT:	WEATHER CONDITIONS:

NAME OF BIRD:

Quantity Spotted: Time seen:

Location seen:	Sights, Activities Sounds When Seen:

Bird actions:

BIRD DESCRIPTION:

species/ features/ markings

NOTES AND INTERESTING EVENTS:

BIRD PHOTO

BIRD SKETCH

DATE:

Day of the week: Time: Season:

AREA NAME:

Location: GPS COORDINATES:

HABITAT:	WEATHER CONDITIONS:

<u>NAME OF BIRD</u>:

Quantity Spotted: Time seen:

Location seen:	Sights, Activities Sounds When Seen:

Bird actions:

BIRD DESCRIPTION:
species/ features/ markings

NOTES AND INTERESTING EVENTS:

_____
_____
_____
_____
_____
_____

BIRD PHOTO

BIRD SKETCH

DATE:

Day of the week: Time: Season:

AREA NAME:

Location: GPS COORDINATES:

HABITAT:	WEATHER CONDITIONS:

NAME OF BIRD:

Quantity Spotted: Time seen:

Location seen:	Sights, Activities Sounds When Seen:

Bird actions:

BIRD DESCRIPTION:

species/ features/ markings

NOTES AND INTERESTING EVENTS:

BIRD PHOTO

BIRD SKETCH

DATE:

Day of the week: Time: Season:

AREA NAME:

Location: GPS COORDINATES:

HABITAT:	WEATHER CONDITIONS:

NAME OF BIRD:

Quantity Spotted: Time seen:

Location seen:	Sights, Activities Sounds When Seen:

Bird actions:

BIRD DESCRIPTION:

species/ features/ markings

NOTES AND INTERESTING EVENTS:

_____
_____
_____
_____
_____
_____

BIRD PHOTO

BIRD SKETCH

DATE:

Day of the week: Time: Season:

AREA NAME:

Location: GPS COORDINATES:

HABITAT:	WEATHER CONDITIONS:

NAME OF BIRD:

Quantity Spotted: Time seen:

Location seen:	Sights, Activities Sounds When Seen:

Bird actions:

_____

_____

_____

_____

_____

BIRD DESCRIPTION:

species/ features/ markings

_____

_____

_____

_____

_____

_____

NOTES AND INTERESTING EVENTS:

BIRD PHOTO

BIRD SKETCH

DATE:

Day of the week: Time: Season:

AREA NAME:

Location: GPS COORDINATES:

HABITAT:	WEATHER CONDITIONS:

NAME OF BIRD:

Quantity Spotted: Time seen:

Location seen:	Sights, Activities Sounds When Seen:

Bird actions:

BIRD DESCRIPTION:

species/ features/ markings

NOTES AND INTERESTING EVENTS:

BIRD PHOTO

BIRD SKETCH

DATE:

Day of the week:　　　　　　　Time:　　　　　　Season:

AREA NAME:

Location:　　　　　　　　　　GPS COORDINATES:

HABITAT:	WEATHER CONDITIONS:

<u>NAME OF BIRD</u>:

Quantity Spotted:　　　　　　　Time seen:

Location seen:	Sights, Activities Sounds When Seen:

Bird actions:

BIRD DESCRIPTION:

species/ features/ markings

NOTES AND INTERESTING EVENTS:

BIRD PHOTO

BIRD SKETCH

DATE:

Day of the week: Time: Season:

AREA NAME:

Location: GPS COORDINATES:

HABITAT:	WEATHER CONDITIONS:

<u>NAME OF BIRD</u>:

Quantity Spotted: Time seen:

Location seen:	Sights, Activities Sounds When Seen:

Bird actions:

BIRD DESCRIPTION:

species/ features/ markings

NOTES AND INTERESTING EVENTS:

_____
_____
_____
_____
_____
_____

BIRD PHOTO

BIRD SKETCH

DATE:

Day of the week: Time: Season:

AREA NAME:

Location: GPS COORDINATES:

HABITAT:	WEATHER CONDITIONS:

NAME OF BIRD:

Quantity Spotted: Time seen:

Location seen:	Sights, Activities Sounds When Seen:

Bird actions:

_____

_____

_____

_____

_____

BIRD DESCRIPTION:

species/ features/ markings

_____

_____

_____

_____

_____

_____

NOTES AND INTERESTING EVENTS:

_____
_____
_____
_____
_____
_____

BIRD PHOTO

BIRD SKETCH

DATE:

Day of the week: Time: Season:

AREA NAME:

Location: GPS COORDINATES:

HABITAT:	**WEATHER CONDITIONS:**

NAME OF BIRD:

Quantity Spotted: Time seen:

Location seen:	Sights, Activities Sounds When Seen:

Bird actions:

BIRD DESCRIPTION:

species/ features/ markings

NOTES AND INTERESTING EVENTS:

_____
_____
_____
_____
_____
_____

BIRD PHOTO

BIRD SKETCH

DATE:

Day of the week: Time: Season:

AREA NAME:

Location: GPS COORDINATES:

HABITAT:	WEATHER CONDITIONS:

<u>NAME OF BIRD</u>:

Quantity Spotted: Time seen:

Location seen:	Sights, Activities Sounds When Seen:

Bird actions:

_____

_____

_____

_____

_____

BIRD DESCRIPTION:

species/ features/ markings

_____

_____

_____

_____

_____

_____

_____

NOTES AND INTERESTING EVENTS:

BIRD PHOTO

BIRD SKETCH

DATE:

Day of the week: Time: Season:

AREA NAME:

Location: GPS COORDINATES:

HABITAT:	WEATHER CONDITIONS:

NAME OF BIRD:

Quantity Spotted: Time seen:

Location seen:	Sights, Activities Sounds When Seen:

Bird actions:

_____
_____
_____
_____
_____

BIRD DESCRIPTION:

species/ features/ markings

_____
_____
_____
_____
_____
_____

NOTES AND INTERESTING EVENTS:

BIRD PHOTO

BIRD SKETCH

DATE:

Day of the week: Time: Season:

AREA NAME:

Location: GPS COORDINATES:

HABITAT:	WEATHER CONDITIONS:

NAME OF BIRD:

Quantity Spotted: Time seen:

Location seen:	Sights, Activities Sounds When Seen:

Bird actions:

_____

_____

_____

_____

_____

BIRD DESCRIPTION:

species/ features/ markings

_____

_____

_____

_____

_____

_____

_____

_____

NOTES AND INTERESTING EVENTS:

BIRD PHOTO

BIRD SKETCH

DATE:

Day of the week: Time: Season:

AREA NAME:

Location: GPS COORDINATES:

HABITAT:	WEATHER CONDITIONS:

NAME OF BIRD:

Quantity Spotted: Time seen:

Location seen:	Sights, Activities Sounds When Seen:

Bird actions:

BIRD DESCRIPTION:

species/ features/ markings

NOTES AND INTERESTING EVENTS:

BIRD PHOTO

BIRD SKETCH

DATE:

Day of the week: Time: Season:

AREA NAME:

Location: GPS COORDINATES:

HABITAT:	WEATHER CONDITIONS:

NAME OF BIRD:

Quantity Spotted: Time seen:

Location seen:	Sights, Activities Sounds When Seen:

Bird actions:

BIRD DESCRIPTION:

species/ features/ markings

NOTES AND INTERESTING EVENTS:

BIRD PHOTO

BIRD SKETCH

DATE:

Day of the week: Time: Season:

AREA NAME:

Location: GPS COORDINATES:

HABITAT:	WEATHER CONDITIONS:

NAME OF BIRD:

Quantity Spotted: Time seen:

Location seen:	Sights, Activities Sounds When Seen:

Bird actions:

BIRD DESCRIPTION:

species/ features/ markings

NOTES AND INTERESTING EVENTS:

_____
_____
_____
_____
_____
_____
_____

BIRD PHOTO

BIRD SKETCH

DATE:

Day of the week: Time: Season:

AREA NAME:

Location: GPS COORDINATES:

HABITAT:	WEATHER CONDITIONS:

NAME OF BIRD:

Quantity Spotted: Time seen:

Location seen:	Sights, Activities Sounds When Seen:

Bird actions:

BIRD DESCRIPTION:
species/ features/ markings

NOTES AND INTERESTING EVENTS:

BIRD PHOTO

BIRD SKETCH

DATE:

Day of the week: Time: Season:

AREA NAME:

Location: GPS COORDINATES:

HABITAT:	WEATHER CONDITIONS:

NAME OF BIRD:

Quantity Spotted: Time seen:

Location seen:	Sights, Activities Sounds When Seen:

Bird actions:

BIRD DESCRIPTION:

species/ features/ markings

NOTES AND INTERESTING EVENTS:

BIRD PHOTO

BIRD SKETCH

DATE:

Day of the week: Time: Season:

AREA NAME:

Location: GPS COORDINATES:

HABITAT:	WEATHER CONDITIONS:

NAME OF BIRD:

Quantity Spotted: Time seen:

Location seen:	Sights, Activities Sounds When Seen:

Bird actions:

BIRD DESCRIPTION:

species/ features/ markings

NOTES AND INTERESTING EVENTS:

BIRD PHOTO

BIRD SKETCH

DATE:

Day of the week: Time: Season:

AREA NAME:

Location: GPS COORDINATES:

HABITAT:	WEATHER CONDITIONS:

<u>NAME OF BIRD</u>:

Quantity Spotted: Time seen:

Location seen:	Sights, Activities Sounds When Seen:

Bird actions:

_____

_____

_____

_____

BIRD DESCRIPTION:

species/ features/ markings

_____

_____

_____

_____

NOTES AND INTERESTING EVENTS:

BIRD PHOTO

BIRD SKETCH

DATE:

Day of the week: Time: Season:

AREA NAME:

Location: GPS COORDINATES:

HABITAT:	WEATHER CONDITIONS:

NAME OF BIRD:

Quantity Spotted: Time seen:

Location seen:	Sights, Activities Sounds When Seen:

Bird actions:

BIRD DESCRIPTION:

species/ features/ markings

NOTES AND INTERESTING EVENTS:

_____

_____

_____

_____

_____

_____

BIRD PHOTO

BIRD SKETCH

DATE:

Day of the week: Time: Season:

AREA NAME:

Location: GPS COORDINATES:

HABITAT:	WEATHER CONDITIONS:

NAME OF BIRD:

Quantity Spotted: Time seen:

Location seen:	Sights, Activities Sounds When Seen:

Bird actions:

BIRD DESCRIPTION:

species/ features/ markings

NOTES AND INTERESTING EVENTS:

BIRD PHOTO

BIRD SKETCH

DATE:

Day of the week: Time: Season:

AREA NAME:

Location: GPS COORDINATES:

HABITAT:	WEATHER CONDITIONS:

NAME OF BIRD:

Quantity Spotted: Time seen:

Location seen:	Sights, Activities Sounds When Seen:

Bird actions:

BIRD DESCRIPTION:

species/ features/ markings

NOTES AND INTERESTING EVENTS:

_____

_____

_____

_____

_____

_____

BIRD PHOTO

BIRD SKETCH

DATE:

Day of the week: Time: Season:

AREA NAME:

Location: GPS COORDINATES:

HABITAT:	WEATHER CONDITIONS:

NAME OF BIRD:

Quantity Spotted: Time seen:

Location seen:	Sights, Activities Sounds When Seen:

Bird actions:

BIRD DESCRIPTION:

species/ features/ markings

NOTES AND INTERESTING EVENTS:

_____
_____
_____
_____
_____
_____

BIRD PHOTO

BIRD SKETCH

DATE:

Day of the week: Time: Season:

AREA NAME:

Location: GPS COORDINATES:

HABITAT:	WEATHER CONDITIONS:

NAME OF BIRD:

Quantity Spotted: Time seen:

Location seen:	Sights, Activities Sounds When Seen:

Bird actions:

BIRD DESCRIPTION:

species/ features/ markings

NOTES AND INTERESTING EVENTS:

_____

_____

_____

_____

_____

_____

BIRD PHOTO

BIRD SKETCH

DATE:

Day of the week: Time: Season:

AREA NAME:

Location: GPS COORDINATES:

HABITAT:	WEATHER CONDITIONS:

<u>NAME OF BIRD</u>:

Quantity Spotted: Time seen:

Location seen:	Sights, Activities Sounds When Seen:

Bird actions:

_____
_____
_____
_____
_____

BIRD DESCRIPTION:

species/ features/ markings

_____
_____
_____
_____
_____
_____

NOTES AND INTERESTING EVENTS:

BIRD PHOTO

BIRD SKETCH

DATE:

Day of the week: Time: Season:

AREA NAME:

Location: GPS COORDINATES:

HABITAT:	WEATHER CONDITIONS:

NAME OF BIRD:

Quantity Spotted: Time seen:

Location seen:	Sights, Activities Sounds When Seen:

Bird actions:

BIRD DESCRIPTION:

species/ features/ markings

NOTES AND INTERESTING EVENTS:

_____
_____
_____
_____
_____
_____

BIRD PHOTO

BIRD SKETCH

DATE:

Day of the week: Time: Season:

AREA NAME:

Location: GPS COORDINATES:

HABITAT:	WEATHER CONDITIONS:

NAME OF BIRD:

Quantity Spotted: Time seen:

Location seen:	Sights, Activities Sounds When Seen:

Bird actions:

BIRD DESCRIPTION:

species/ features/ markings

NOTES AND INTERESTING EVENTS:

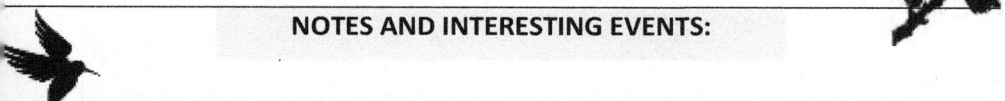

_____
_____
_____
_____
_____
_____

BIRD PHOTO

BIRD SKETCH

DATE:

Day of the week: Time: Season:

AREA NAME:

Location: GPS COORDINATES:

HABITAT:	WEATHER CONDITIONS:

NAME OF BIRD:

Quantity Spotted: Time seen:

Location seen:	Sights, Activities Sounds When Seen:

Bird actions:

_____

_____

_____

_____

_____

BIRD DESCRIPTION:

species/ features/ markings

_____

_____

_____

_____

_____

_____

NOTES AND INTERESTING EVENTS:

BIRD PHOTO

BIRD SKETCH

DATE:

Day of the week: Time: Season:

AREA NAME:

Location: GPS COORDINATES:

HABITAT:	WEATHER CONDITIONS:

<u>NAME OF BIRD</u>:

Quantity Spotted: Time seen:

Location seen:	Sights, Activities Sounds When Seen:

Bird actions:

BIRD DESCRIPTION:
species/ features/ markings

NOTES AND INTERESTING EVENTS:

BIRD PHOTO

BIRD SKETCH

DATE:

Day of the week: Time: Season:

AREA NAME:

Location: GPS COORDINATES:

HABITAT:	WEATHER CONDITIONS:

<u>NAME OF BIRD</u>:

Quantity Spotted: Time seen:

Location seen:	Sights, Activities Sounds When Seen:

Bird actions:

BIRD DESCRIPTION:
species/ features/ markings

NOTES AND INTERESTING EVENTS:

BIRD PHOTO

BIRD SKETCH

DATE:

Day of the week: Time: Season:

AREA NAME:

Location: GPS COORDINATES:

HABITAT:	WEATHER CONDITIONS:

NAME OF BIRD:

Quantity Spotted: Time seen:

Location seen:	Sights, Activities Sounds When Seen:

Bird actions:

BIRD DESCRIPTION:

species/ features/ markings

NOTES AND INTERESTING EVENTS:

_____
_____
_____
_____
_____
_____

BIRD PHOTO

BIRD SKETCH

DATE:

Day of the week: Time: Season:

AREA NAME:

Location: GPS COORDINATES:

HABITAT:	WEATHER CONDITIONS:

NAME OF BIRD:

Quantity Spotted: Time seen:

Location seen:	Sights, Activities Sounds When Seen:

Bird actions:

BIRD DESCRIPTION:

species/ features/ markings

NOTES AND INTERESTING EVENTS:

_____
_____
_____
_____
_____
_____

BIRD PHOTO

BIRD SKETCH

DATE:

Day of the week: Time: Season:

AREA NAME:

Location: GPS COORDINATES:

HABITAT:	WEATHER CONDITIONS:

NAME OF BIRD:

Quantity Spotted: Time seen:

Location seen:	Sights, Activities Sounds When Seen:

Bird actions:

_____

_____

_____

_____

_____

BIRD DESCRIPTION:

species/ features/ markings

_____

_____

_____

_____

_____

NOTES AND INTERESTING EVENTS:

BIRD PHOTO

BIRD SKETCH

DATE:

Day of the week: Time: Season:

AREA NAME:

Location: GPS COORDINATES:

HABITAT:	WEATHER CONDITIONS:

<u>NAME OF BIRD</u>:

Quantity Spotted: Time seen:

Location seen:	Sights, Activities Sounds When Seen:

Bird actions:

BIRD DESCRIPTION:
species/ features/ markings

NOTES AND INTERESTING EVENTS:

_____

_____

_____

_____

_____

_____

BIRD PHOTO

BIRD SKETCH

DATE:

Day of the week: Time: Season:

AREA NAME:

Location: GPS COORDINATES:

HABITAT:	WEATHER CONDITIONS:

NAME OF BIRD:

Quantity Spotted: Time seen:

Location seen:	Sights, Activities Sounds When Seen:

Bird actions:

BIRD DESCRIPTION:

species/ features/ markings

NOTES AND INTERESTING EVENTS:

BIRD PHOTO

BIRD SKETCH

DATE:

Day of the week: Time: Season:

AREA NAME:

Location: GPS COORDINATES:

HABITAT:	WEATHER CONDITIONS:

NAME OF BIRD:

Quantity Spotted: Time seen:

Location seen:	Sights, Activities Sounds When Seen:

Bird actions:

BIRD DESCRIPTION:

species/ features/ markings

NOTES AND INTERESTING EVENTS:

_____
_____
_____
_____
_____
_____

BIRD PHOTO

BIRD SKETCH

DATE:

Day of the week: Time: Season:

AREA NAME:

Location: GPS COORDINATES:

HABITAT:	WEATHER CONDITIONS:

<u>NAME OF BIRD</u>:

Quantity Spotted: Time seen:

Location seen:	Sights, Activities Sounds When Seen:

Bird actions:

_____

_____

_____

_____

_____

BIRD DESCRIPTION:

species/ features/ markings

_____

_____

_____

_____

_____

NOTES AND INTERESTING EVENTS:

_____

_____

_____

_____

_____

_____

BIRD PHOTO

BIRD SKETCH

DATE:

Day of the week: Time: Season:

AREA NAME:

Location: GPS COORDINATES:

HABITAT:	WEATHER CONDITIONS:

NAME OF BIRD:

Quantity Spotted: Time seen:

Location seen:	Sights, Activities Sounds When Seen:

Bird actions:

_____
_____
_____
_____
_____

BIRD DESCRIPTION:

species/ features/ markings

_____
_____
_____
_____
_____
_____

NOTES AND INTERESTING EVENTS:

BIRD PHOTO

BIRD SKETCH

DATE:

Day of the week: Time: Season:

AREA NAME:

Location: GPS COORDINATES:

HABITAT:	WEATHER CONDITIONS:

NAME OF BIRD:

Quantity Spotted: Time seen:

Location seen:	Sights, Activities Sounds When Seen:

Bird actions:

BIRD DESCRIPTION:

species/ features/ markings

NOTES AND INTERESTING EVENTS:

_____
_____
_____
_____
_____
_____
_____

BIRD PHOTO

BIRD SKETCH

DATE:

Day of the week: Time: Season:

AREA NAME:

Location: GPS COORDINATES:

HABITAT:	WEATHER CONDITIONS:

NAME OF BIRD:

Quantity Spotted: Time seen:

Location seen:	Sights, Activities Sounds When Seen:

Bird actions:

BIRD DESCRIPTION:

species/ features/ markings

NOTES AND INTERESTING EVENTS:

BIRD PHOTO

BIRD SKETCH

DATE:

Day of the week: Time: Season:

AREA NAME:

Location: GPS COORDINATES:

HABITAT:	WEATHER CONDITIONS:

<u>NAME OF BIRD</u>:

Quantity Spotted: Time seen:

Location seen:	Sights, Activities Sounds When Seen:

Bird actions:

BIRD DESCRIPTION:
species/ features/ markings

NOTES AND INTERESTING EVENTS:

BIRD PHOTO

BIRD SKETCH

DATE:

Day of the week: Time: Season:

AREA NAME:

Location: GPS COORDINATES:

HABITAT:	WEATHER CONDITIONS:

NAME OF BIRD:

Quantity Spotted: Time seen:

Location seen:	Sights, Activities Sounds When Seen:

Bird actions:

BIRD DESCRIPTION:
species/ features/ markings

NOTES AND INTERESTING EVENTS:

_____
_____
_____
_____
_____
_____

BIRD PHOTO

BIRD SKETCH

DATE:

Day of the week: Time: Season:

AREA NAME:

Location: GPS COORDINATES:

HABITAT:	WEATHER CONDITIONS:

NAME OF BIRD:

Quantity Spotted: Time seen:

Location seen:	Sights, Activities Sounds When Seen:

Bird actions:

_____

_____

_____

_____

_____

BIRD DESCRIPTION:

species/ features/ markings

_____

_____

_____

_____

_____

_____

NOTES AND INTERESTING EVENTS:

_____
_____
_____
_____
_____
_____

BIRD PHOTO

BIRD SKETCH

DATE:

Day of the week: Time: Season:

AREA NAME:

Location: GPS COORDINATES:

HABITAT:	WEATHER CONDITIONS:

<u>NAME OF BIRD</u>:

Quantity Spotted: Time seen:

Location seen:	Sights, Activities Sounds When Seen:

Bird actions:

BIRD DESCRIPTION:

species/ features/ markings

NOTES AND INTERESTING EVENTS:

BIRD PHOTO

BIRD SKETCH

DATE:

Day of the week: Time: Season:

AREA NAME:

Location: GPS COORDINATES:

HABITAT:	WEATHER CONDITIONS:

NAME OF BIRD:

Quantity Spotted: Time seen:

Location seen:	Sights, Activities Sounds When Seen:

Bird actions:

BIRD DESCRIPTION:

species/ features/ markings

NOTES AND INTERESTING EVENTS:

BIRD PHOTO

BIRD SKETCH

DATE:

Day of the week: Time: Season:

AREA NAME:

Location: GPS COORDINATES:

HABITAT:	WEATHER CONDITIONS:

<u>NAME OF BIRD</u>:

Quantity Spotted: Time seen:

Location seen:	Sights, Activities Sounds When Seen:

Bird actions:

_____
_____
_____
_____
_____

BIRD DESCRIPTION:
species/ features/ markings

_____
_____
_____
_____
_____
_____

NOTES AND INTERESTING EVENTS:

BIRD PHOTO

BIRD SKETCH

DATE:

Day of the week: Time: Season:

AREA NAME:

Location: GPS COORDINATES:

HABITAT:	WEATHER CONDITIONS:

NAME OF BIRD:

Quantity Spotted: Time seen:

Location seen:	Sights, Activities Sounds When Seen:

Bird actions:

BIRD DESCRIPTION:

species/ features/ markings

_____
_____
_____
_____
_____
_____
_____

BIRD PHOTO

BIRD SKETCH

DATE:

Day of the week: Time: Season:

AREA NAME:

Location: GPS COORDINATES:

HABITAT:	WEATHER CONDITIONS:

NAME OF BIRD:

Quantity Spotted: Time seen:

Location seen:	Sights, Activities Sounds When Seen:

Bird actions:

BIRD DESCRIPTION:

species/ features/ markings

NOTES AND INTERESTING EVENTS:

BIRD PHOTO

BIRD SKETCH

DATE:

Day of the week: Time: Season:

AREA NAME:

Location: GPS COORDINATES:

HABITAT:	WEATHER CONDITIONS:

<u>NAME OF BIRD:</u>

Quantity Spotted: Time seen:

Location seen:	Sights, Activities Sounds When Seen:

Bird actions:

_____

_____

_____

_____

_____

BIRD DESCRIPTION:

species/ features/ markings

_____

_____

_____

_____

_____

NOTES AND INTERESTING EVENTS:

BIRD PHOTO

BIRD SKETCH

DATE:

Day of the week: Time: Season:

AREA NAME:

Location: GPS COORDINATES:

HABITAT:	WEATHER CONDITIONS:

NAME OF BIRD:

Quantity Spotted: Time seen:

Location seen:	Sights, Activities Sounds When Seen:

Bird actions:

_____
_____
_____
_____
_____

BIRD DESCRIPTION:

species/ features/ markings

_____
_____
_____
_____
_____
_____
_____

NOTES AND INTERESTING EVENTS:

BIRD PHOTO

BIRD SKETCH

DATE:

Day of the week: Time: Season:

AREA NAME:

Location: GPS COORDINATES:

HABITAT:	WEATHER CONDITIONS:

NAME OF BIRD:

Quantity Spotted: Time seen:

Location seen:	Sights, Activities Sounds When Seen:

Bird actions:

BIRD DESCRIPTION:

species/ features/ markings

Printed in Great Britain
by Amazon